Facts About the Spix Macaw (Blue Macaw)

The Spix Macaw Up Close

By Lisa Strattin

© 2016 Lisa Strattin

Facts for Kids Picture Books by Lisa Strattin

Red Kangaroo, Vol 84

Kinkajou, Vol 85

Klipspringer, Vol 86

Kudu Antelope, Vol 87

Bushbaby, Vol 88

Amur Leopard, Vol 89

Barbet Dog, Vol 90

Lilac Breasted Roller, Vol 91

Little Blue Penguin, Vol 92

Big Brown Bat, Vol 93

Sign Up for New Release Emails Here

http://lisastrattin.com/subscribe-here

Join the KidCrafts Monthly Program Here

http://kidcraftsbylisa.com

All rights reserved. No part of this book may be reproduced by any means whatsoever without the written permission from the author, except brief portions quoted for purpose of review.

All information in this book has been carefully researched and checked for factual accuracy. However, the author and publisher makes no warranty, express or implied, that the information contained herein is appropriate for every individual, situation or purpose and assume no responsibility for errors or omissions. The reader assumes the risk and full responsibility for all actions, and the author will not be held responsible for any loss or damage, whether consequential, incidental, special or otherwise, that may result from the information presented in this book.

I have relied on my own observations as well as many different sources for this book and I have done my best to check facts and give credit where it is due. In the event that any material is used without proper permission, please contact me so that the oversight can be corrected.

Contents

INTRODUCTION 7
CHARACTERISTICS OR HABITS 9
APPEARANCE 11
LIFE STAGES 15
LIFE SPAN 17
SIZE 19
HABITAT 21
DIET 22
FRIENDS/ENEMIES 22
SUITABILITY AS PETS 23
BLUE MACAW HAND PUPPET 25
KIDCRAFTS MONTHLY SUBSCRIPTION PROGRAM 26

INTRODUCTION

Spix (blue) macaw is one of the world's rarest birds. Been critically endangered, Macaws were believed to have gone into extinction in the wild because they had not been sighted in the woodlands and creeks of northeast Brazil since 2000. It is as a result of the deforestation in Central and South America, and illegal trapping for black market sales. This extremely rare parrot is being saved by a good number of important captive breeding programs.

COLOR ME

CHARACTERISTICS OR HABITS

These birds are often active during the daytime while they spend their nights beside streams. They are always in pairs or family group. They usually fly slow, deep wing-beat that is reminiscent of bigger macaws; along with their regular call sound 'Kraa-ark.'

COLOR ME

They are shy and can be aggressive when threatened. They are also protective of their eggs and young ones. Being routine-oriented, they maintain a strict schedule, performing their regular activities like; roosting, feeding, nesting, and social interaction at the same time every day. The fact that their routine is predictable made them easy targets for trappers and hunters.

APPEARANCE

This beautiful parrot has delicate blue-grey feathers, fading from the bright blue tail and wings to an ashy-blue crown. The dark grey skin around the eyes has no feathers. Young Spix macaws are typically dark blue in color, but the skin around the eye is pale. The blue feathers turn darker on the wings and the tail. The underparts are more whitish, rather than blue-grey. The under tail plumages are light grey, and the underwing shows pale grey flight feathers.

The pale blue-grey head is different with the darker body. The forehead, cheeks, and ear-coverts are faintly washed blue. The hooked bill is blackish grey. Spix Macaw adults have pale straw-colored eyes, with

COLOR ME

Samba

grey eye-ring and bare dark grey lore. Legs and feet are grey-brown. Though the male and female have so many things in common, the female are slightly smaller than male.

The young ones look like the adults, with slightly darker feathers and rather whitish-grey to a grey bare facial area. It has a shorter tail than adults. Its eyes are dark first, but they become gradually lighter.

COLOR ME

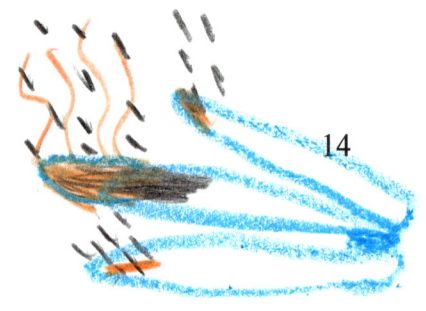

LIFE STAGES   Blu, Bianca, and Bedioz
Blue,

The life of a macaw starts with the hatchery of an egg into a baby bird after one month of incubation in its parents' nest. Juvenile macaws make their first fly out of the nest about three months after hatching. Then after about a year, they leave the nest permanently. Juveniles resemble their parents. The only different is that younger birds have shorter tails and darker eyes.

A young macaw reaches maturation period at the age of 3 to 6 years after hatching then, and it finds a mate. Unlike other kinds of animal, Macaws are monogamous and mate for life. When the female nurtures the eggs in the nest, the male finds food and carries it back to the nest.

15

COLOR ME

Macaws don't mate every year; this is because they live for some decades, though a mating pair may lay some clutches of eggs over a lifetime together. Macaws typically breed between October and April.

LIFE SPAN

There is limited information about the lifespan of this species. However, these humid birds had been said to live between twenty-eight and thirty-five years in the wild, though some live up to fifty years in captivity.

COLOR ME

SIZE

Body Length: 55 - 57 cm

Tail Length: 26 – 38 cm

Wing Length: 25 -30 cm

Average Wingspan: 1 – 20 cm

Weight- The male weighs around 280 – 400g while the female weighs 266 -400g

COLOR ME

HABITAT

Spix macaws inhabit the Caraibeira riparian woodland gallery along seasonal creeks, in the dry scrub zone known as Caatinga, situated along Río Sao Francisco valley, in north-eastern Brazil.

These birds find shelter on Caribbean Trumpet Trees (Tabebuia caraiba or Tabebuia aurea) which grow to 26 feet and are usually covered in bright yellow flowers. These trees provide roosting and nesting opportunities for macaws.

DIET

These birds dine on different fruits (mostly cactus fruit), seed, nuts, leaves, flowers, insect, and snail.

FRIENDS/ENEMIES

The predators of Macaws are human beings, monkeys, and large birds. Due to their brightly colored plumages, macaws are regularly hunted by the tribesman. However, International collaboration is assisting the effort to recover macaw from the verge of extinction.

SUITABILITY AS PETS

Macaws can be kept as a pet. However, the Spix or Blue Macaw is protected in many areas and it might not be legal for you to own one. Macaws are desirable, intelligent and sociable. Nevertheless, there are some things to bear in mind before bringing a macaw into the home. They are very noisy and lively creatures and require a larger amount of attention because they can be destructive. They also have an extended lifespan of over 40 years. Therefore, it is essential to have a home lined up for the bird if it is young. Macaws are sometimes crossbred for the pet trade, altering their colors and genetics.

Please leave me a review here:

http://lisastrattin.com/Review-Vol-16

For more Kindle Downloads Visit Lisa Strattin Author Page on Amazon Author Central

http://amazon.com/author/lisastrattin

To see upcoming titles, visit my website at LisaStrattin.com – all books available on kindle!

http://lisastrattin.com

BLUE MACAW HAND PUPPET

You can get one by copying and pasting this link into your browser: http://lisastrattin.com/spixhandpuppet

KIDCRAFTS MONTHLY SUBSCRIPTION PROGRAM

Receive a Box of Crafts and a Lisa Strattin Full Color Paperback Book Each Month in Your Mailbox!

Get yours by copying and pasting this link into your browser

http://KidCraftsByLisa.com

Printed in Great Britain
by Amazon